W9-BRS-524

ideals®
OLD-FASHIONED

Oh, the days gone by!
Oh, the days gone by!
The music of the laughing lip,
The lustre of the eye;
The childish faith in fairies,
And Aladdin's magic ring —
The simple, soul-reposing, glad
Belief in everything —
When life was like a story
Holding neither sob nor sigh,
In the golden olden glory
Of the days gone by.

James Whitcomb Riley

ISBN 0-8249-1036-2 350

IDEALS — Vol. 42, No. 5 June MCMLXXXV IDEALS (ISSN 0019-137X) is published eight times a year,
February, March, May, June, August, September, November, December
by IDEALS PUBLISHING CORPORATION, 11315 Watertown Plank Road, Milwaukee, Wis. 53226
Second class postage paid at Milwaukee, Wisconsin and additional mailing offices.
Copyright © MCMLXXXV by IDEALS PUBLISHING CORPORATION.
POSTMASTER: Send address changes to Ideals, Post Office Box 2100, Milwaukee, Wis. 53201
All rights reserved. Title IDEALS registered U.S. Patent Office.
Published simultaneously in Canada.

SINGLE ISSUE — $3.50
ONE YEAR SUBSCRIPTION — eight consecutive issues as published — $15.95
TWO YEAR SUBSCRIPTION — sixteen consecutive issues as published — $27.95
Outside U.S.A., add $4.00 per subscription year for postage and handling

IDEALS assumes no responsibility for unsolicited material. Manuscripts will not be returned unless
accompanied with a self-addressed envelope and return postage.

Publisher, Patricia A. Pingry
Editor/Ideals, Kathleen S. Pohl
Managing Editor, Marybeth Owens
Photographic Editor, Gerald Koser
Research Editor, Linda Robinson
Editorial Assistant, Carmen Johnson
Editorial Assistant, Amanda Barrickman
Phototypesetter, Kim Kaczanowski
Staff Artist, Patrick McRae

*Front and
back cover
GINGERBREAD MANSION
Ed Cooper*

Violets for Mother

Hidden down in the meadow grass,
The largest violets grew.
We gathered the fragrant blossoms
Still wet with morning dew.

One by one we added the stems
To the others in our hand,
Till we held bouquets of purple
From the sunny meadowland.

We carried them home so proudly,
Guarding our treasure well,
Touching our cheeks to their petals,
Inhaling their lovely smell.

We presented them to Mother,
As children always will,
And the violets looked so pretty
On the kitchen windowsill.

Harriet Whipple

Photo opposite
GLASS JAR BOUQUET
Karen Tompkins

The Milk House

There used to be an old milk house
Out near the family well.
The house, our special storing place,
Gave off a buttermilk smell.
We kept the walls all whitewashed clean
And daily scrubbed the floor
When we were only little girls —
Now that was quite a chore!
The crocks and jars were in a trough;
The water was pumped in
To keep the cream and cheese so fresh —
The milk our mom would skim.
Then she'd make butter — lots of it —
And some she'd take to sell;
The rest we'd store in that milk house
Out near the family well.

Agnes Finch Whitacre

Spring House

Between the house and barn, the spring house stood:
Moss-embellished stone and aged wood.
Inside, descending rough-hewn granite stairs,
One could dimly make out country wares:
A tub of golden butter, eggs, and cream,
And home-smoked ham suspended from a beam,
Cans of milk sunk deep within the spring,
The cider jug (a large and ice cold thing),
A melon floating, bobbing all about,
As crystal water gurgled from the spout.
The dank and fragrant air I still can smell
Was scented by mint crushed where footsteps fell.
This cherished memory recalls the ways
Of hardy folk who lived in other days.

Ruth B. Field

A Mortifying Mistake

I studied my tables over and over,
   and backward and forward, too;
But I couldn't remember six times nine,
   and I didn't know what to do,
Till Sister told me to play with my doll,
   and not to bother my head.
"If you call her 'Fifty-four' for a while,
   you'll learn it by heart," she said.
So I took my favorite, Mary Ann,
   (though I thought 'twas a dreadful shame
To give such a perfectly lovely child
   such a perfectly horrid name)
And I called her my dear little "Fifty-four"
   a hundred times, till I knew
The answer of six times nine as well as
   the answer of two times two.

Next day Elizabeth Wigglesworth,
   who always acts so proud,
Said, "Six times nine is fifty-two,"
   and I nearly laughed aloud!
But I wished I hadn't when teacher said,
   "Now, Dorothy, tell if you can."
For I thought of my doll and — sakes alive!
   I answered, "*Mary Ann!*"

Anna Maria Pratt

$$2 \times 2 = 5 \quad 3 \times 3 = 7 \quad 1 \times 4 = 2$$

Photo opposite
LITTLE RED SCHOOLHOUSE
Ken Dequaine

McGUFFEY'S FIRST READER

LESSON XLIV

laid	laugh	fleece	school
wait-ed	lamb	Ma-ry	an-i-mal
love	snow	gen-tle	pa-tient-ly

OF THE ECLECTIC SERIES.

MA-RY'S LAMB.

Ma-ry had a lit-tle lamb,
  Its fleece was white as snow,
And ev-er-y where that Ma-ry went,
  The lamb was sure to go.

He went with her to school one day;
  That was a-gainst the rule;
It made the chil-dren laugh and play,
  To see a lamb at school.

So the teach-er turn-ed him out,
  But still he ling-er-ed near,
And wait-ed pa-tient-ly a-bout,
  Till Ma-ry did ap-pear.

And then he ran to her, and laid
  His head up-on her arm,
As if he said; I'm not a-fraid,
  You'll keep me from all harm.

"What makes the lamb love Ma-ry so?"
  The ea-ger chil-dren cry;
"O Ma-ry loves the lamb, you know,"
  The teach-er did re-ply.

"And you, each gen-tle an-i-mal
  To you, for life, may bind,
And make it fol-low at your call,
  If you are al-ways *kind*."

When She Must Go

When she must go, so much will go with her!
　　Stories of country summers, far and bright,
Wisdom of berries, flowers and chestnut bur,
　　And songs to comfort babies in the night;

Old legends and their meanings, half-lost tunes,
　　Wise craftsmanship in all the household ways,
And roses taught to flower in summer noons,
　　And children taught the shaping of good days;

A heart still steadfast, stable, that can know
　　A son's first loss, a daughter's first heartbreak,
And say to them, "This, too, shall pass and go;
　　This is not all!" while anguished for their sake;

Courage to cling to when the day is lost,
　　Love to come back to when all love grows cold,
Quiet from tumult; hearth fire from the frost.
　　Oh, must she ever go, and we be old?

Margaret Widdemer

Photo opposite
SUMMER FUN
Bob Higbee
Berg & Associates

An Awful Lot to Fishin'

There's an awful lot to fishin'
   Besides your line and pole.
With the speckled beauties hidin'
   In some cool, deep hole.
There's the voices of the waters
   That go laughing, bounding by,
Showing crystals in the sunlight,
   Reflecting azure from the sky.

There's the frolic of the rapids,
   Coming, gurgling, bubbling on;
There's the stillness of the deep pools
   Where the fishes come to spawn.
There's the cricket's steady chirping
   From his home beneath a stone;
From the flowers in the meadow
   Comes the honeybees' soft drone.

The chipmunk eyes you shyly
   From his safely distant log,
And right down here below you
   Is a silent, bright-green frog.
The catbird comes to scold you
   From his perch upon a limb,
As he peers down at the minnows,
   Just a-learnin' how to swim.

You hear the rasping locust
   As you sit there in the sun;
You just feel a part of nature
   And all the days are one.
You look down in the water
   At the shining stone and sand;
You praise the God that made you
   And bless the guidance of His hand.

You plumb forget your fishin'
   And you never get a bite,
But the silence deep within you
   Makes you feel that that's all right.
What! You say that that ain't fishin'?
   Well, maybe that is true,
But I say the man that does it
   Don't go home a-feelin' blue.

I'll admit that there's a thriller
   In the singing of your reel,
But it don't compare in glory
   To the things you hear and feel.
This chumming up with Nature's
   The salvation of your soul.
There's an awful lot to fishin'
   Besides your line and pole.

R. C. Calloway

Where Wild Roses Grow

I wish I could go back and be
A little girl once more —
Have my father read to me
Of history and folklore,
Take piano lessons from Miss Rose,
Tell jokes to cousin Mark,
Play dress up in my mama's clothes,
Chase fireflies after dark,

Wear white organdy to Sunday school,
Play chess with Uncle Ray,
Sit on Grandpa's milking stool,
Gather eggs from nests of hay.
But childhood innocence is over;
All the best is lost to me —
Wild roses grow in scented clover —
But only in my memory.

Elsie Mae Watkins

Photo opposite
PURPLE ROSE
Alice & Frank Rodziewicz

Old-Fashioned Dolls

They have been friends and confidants, playmates and soul mates, the mirrors of our feelings and the objects of our youthful attentions.

Looking back through the fragments of childhood that remain in the dusty corners of our hearts, there are few among us who could not admit to finding there a memory of at least one special doll, one who kept our secrets loyally or played a part in our imaginary rescues and adventures.

From commoners to kings, dolls have been a universal factor in childhood since the dawn of man. Through the ages, they have reflected styles and religion, values and societies. No dolls have been found in prehistoric graves, probably because they were made of perishable materials, but a fragment of an alabaster doll with movable arms has been recovered from ancient Babylonian times.

Little is known about the dolls of the Middle Ages — only a few small figures, including some of knights, survive — but that period brought the development and veneration of the creche, or Nativity scene, with figures of the Holy Family and the Magi. As the creche's popularity grew in Catholic Europe during the seventeenth and eighteenth centuries, Protestant Europe developed an affinity for elaborate dollhouses instead.

"Fashion dolls" evolved in the late fourteenth century, long before Barbie ever wore an evening gown to the prom with Ken, as a way for Parisian dressmakers to send the latest styles from the French court to the Queen of England. Paris, predictably, became a leading producer of the fashion dolls.

American pioneer children often played with dolls made from the simple materials that figured into their everyday struggle for survival — there were rag dolls, of course, centuries before Raggedy Ann made her appearance, and cornhusk dolls that had to be stored out of the reach of hungry mice. "Nuthead" dolls, with bodies of rags or cornhusks, were meant to be expendable — when children grew bored with these playthings, the decorated "heads" could be cracked and eaten.

Dollmakers have been on a never-ending quest to make their works more lifelike since the days of antiquity. Dolls with limbs that could be moved predate Christianity. Crudely movable limbs fastened to the body with pins were followed by those with increasingly more refined and flexible joints. Human hair began to be used, and then synthetic fibers that could hold up under repeated washings. Eyes were counterweighted to simulate "sleep" when a doll was prone, and, of course, dolls that drank and wet and walked and crawled couldn't be too far behind. Talking dolls were developed as early as the 1800s — "Mama" and "Papa" were favorite expressions — and in 1889, Thomas A. Edison invented a doll that used a miniature phonograph to sing nursery songs.

Little Shirley Temple, all smiles and golden ringlets in her screen appearances, proved a very popular celebrity to model dolls after, but this was not strictly a twentieth century dollmaking practice — even George Washington turned up in a form children could play with in the late 1700s. Raggedy Ann and Andy, based on children's books by Johnny Gruelle, have been a favorite in the United States for generations.

But regardless of who they resemble or how they are packaged and marketed from one generation to the next, dolls continue to be an enduring symbol of childhood, and remain in the heart of the child within us.

Mary T. Wagner

Old-Fashioned Attic

The door always squeaks just a little
Whenever a child turns the knob;
The stairs are both narrow and so steep
That climbing's a difficult job.

There're long empty alleys for running
With noisily pounding feet;
There're dark, little cubbies for hiding
And hollows where echo sounds meet;

Some large boxes bulging with tinsel
Join flags from the Fourth of July;
There are bundles of ribbon-tied letters,
And trunks of old clothes to try.

Oh, lucky the child with an attic
And memories from yesterday —
Adventure and often enchantment
Await him when he comes to play.

Ruth J. Jorgensen

Old Rooms

I love old rooms where memories lie
In paneled walls and chimney nooks,
Where lamplight bares an ancient hearth
And rows of near forgotten books;
Where candlesticks of pewter shine
With their quaint, time-burnished gleam,
And olden tales are hummed along
To resurrect a silent dream.

I love old rooms where memories live
To recreate another day,
Where old wood stoves still rule supreme
And hints of sweet aromas stay;
Where candleglow still wakes to dance
Upon the walls and rough-hewn beams,
And mantel clocks record the hours
Of peace and sweet rememberings.

For old rooms seem to smile anew
Within the warmth of candleglow,
And time is but a dream that stayed
To whisper of the long ago.

Joy Belle Burgess

When Mother Read to Me

At evening when the fires were lit,
When lights were burning bright,
I snuggled up in Mother's lap,
A carefree little sprite.
My head I pillowed on her breast,
From cares my mind was free;
I found the moments so divine
When Mother read to me.

She read me tales of far-off lands,
Of pretty fairies, gay,
And of the goblins that come round
On every Halloween Day.
I was carried on a ship to Spain
Or to a mountain high
Where I could touch the fleecy clouds
That drifted so idly by.

I sailed the wild, tempestuous sea,
And scaled Mount Shasta's height;
I even hunted wild elephants
In Africa at night.
Oh! I'd go clear around the world
From Mother's lap . . . you see
I was a brave adventurer
When Mother read to me.

Mrs. Paul E. King

Getting Ready for Town

The butter is in the firkin, and the eggs
Are stowed behind the farmer's nervous legs,
Which seem strange to him in their Sunday pair
Of trousers, full of lint and prickly hair.
The cat is locked up in the lower shed.
The small boy misses the wind upon his head;
It is his hat, he suddenly remembers.
The teakettle has put out the last red embers
In the stove. The farmer's wife has been
Her third and last time back to put the tin
Of cookies in a place the hired man
Can see it without looking, and the can
Of coffee by it, though the man may be
Too lazy for it and may drink cold tea.
The farmer's wife has put the spun-yarn loop
With the key upon it on the stoop
Under the big white shell, and she climbs in.

Her husband rubs the place below his chin
The razor did not reach. It's out of sight.
He glances round, his deep eyes fill with light
To see how well his two boys look, dressed neat;
They will show him off to folks upstreet.
It does not matter if his coat is worn
Or that his collar at the back is torn:
The trousers prickling at his knees are new;
His wife's dressed up all fine, so are his two
Boys in back. He takes a last quick look
At everything — his house, his trees, his brook.
He feels in for the wallet at his side.
They all sit up, excited for the ride.

Robert P. Tristram Coffin

General Store

Someday I'm going to have a store
With a tinkly bell hung over the door,
With real glass cases and counters wide
And drawers, all spilly with things inside.
There'll be a little of everything:
Bolts of calico; balls of string;
Jars of peppermint; tins of tea;
Pots and kettles and crockery;

Seeds in packets; scissors bright;
Kegs of sugar, brown and white;
Sarsaparilla for picnic lunches,
Bananas and rubber boots in bunches.
I'll fix the window and dust each shelf,
And take the money in all myself.
It will be my store and I will say:
"What can I do for you today?"

Rachel Field

From the book TAXIS AND TOADSTOOLS by Rachel Field. Copyright 1926
by Rachel Field. Published by Doubleday & Co., Inc.

Grandma's Button Box

My grandma was a seamstress;
She earned her wage that way,
And though she's long retired,
She sews most every day.
She always carries with her
A thimble and some thread,
A tiny pair of scissors,
And a needle that she says

Will come in very handy
In case, by some surprise,
The need to do some mending
Might suddenly arise.
My grandma has some things
She's piled up through the years —
Odds and ends of fabrics,
Old patterns she holds dear.

But the things she has the most of,
Or so it seems to me,
Are buttons by the boxful
Which she adds to constantly.
"I need a button sewed on!"
She often hears us say,
And off to get her button box,
She bustles straight away.

It seems she has a million
Of every size and hue;
She even has some buttons
That are shaped like little cubes!
While some of them are wooden,
There are others made of brass,
And some are even antique,
I think made out of glass.

I'm sure that there's a story
For each button in that box,
Recalling all the things she's made
From coats to party frocks.
So, if you need a button,
Don't buy one in a shop —
Until you first have looked inside
My grandma's button box.

Coleen L. Lewis

Great-Grandmother's Kitchen

Her kitchen was plain. No tile on its wall
To make it attractive; no, not at all!
Nor was any inlaid linoleum there,
For counter and flooring were spotlessly bare.
She had no time-savers at all, big or little,
In this old-fashioned room with its coal and
   its scuttle,
But she rubbed and she scrubbed until
   everything shone,
And somehow she gave it a charm all its own.

Her time was not spent over fancy hors d'oeuvres,
But her cupboards were filled with all sorts
   of preserves,
And always there hovered a scent tantalizing
That savored of things that were most appetizing:
A pleasing aroma of things stocked ahead,
Or a soft pungent odor of freshly baked bread,
Of doughnuts and gingerbread, apples and spice,
And somehow her kitchen was ever so nice!

Ruth Linnea Erickson

The Flour Bin

I remember that our pantry
Held a most essential thing —
We could not have done without it —
My mother's flour bin.

It was heavy, made of hardwood,
Painted gray, of goodly size,
Built to hold the main ingredient
For biscuits, breads, and pies.

Mother baked an awful lot then,
With her bread a specialty,
And a buttered slice with peach jam
Is my favorite memory.

Father often checked the flour bin
To see if it might show,
That with many mouths to feed,
We had run a little low.

And we all knew luck was with us
If, when travelers dropped in,
There was ham out in the smokehouse
And some flour in the bin.

Margaret Neel

Homespun Song

With eyes like saucers, I recall,
I watched the spinning wheel,
Its shadow whirling on the wall,
The distaff's dizzy reel.
The farmer's wife stepped to and fro
While busy was her hand,
Feeding wool in steady flow
Which came out in a strand.
Old spinning wheel in rhythmic time
Kept turning, whisp'ring round
With its ceaseless creaking rhyme —
A hypnotizing sound.

Ruth B. Field

Photo opposite
SPINNING WOOL
H. Armstrong Roberts

To an Old Farmhouse

"I like old houses that are weather-stained,
   Whose doorsteps sag beneath their weight of years,
Old walls that echo back with softened tone
   The laughter that we know, the sound of tears.

Old wooden beds that glow with luster dim,
   Old rooms where birth and death have often trod,
Old stairways echoing back the tired feet,
   Like the rain that beats against the quiet sod.

Old treasured quilts with tiny stitches made,
　Bits of gay dresses that our mothers had.
Old pictures in an album gray and dim,
　A little blue-eyed boy that once was Dad.

Old roomy kitchens steeped in fragrant food,
　The shining stove, its welcome, gracious cheer,
Old cellars made of stone with crib and bin,
　Storing with pride the harvests of the year.

Old parlors hushed and clean, stiff chairs arrayed
　In stately rows beside the shining wall,
A feather wreath, a gaudy painted fan,
　The stilted splendor of a Chinese doll.

Old homes that breathe of peace and quiet hours,
　That we in happy dreams may see again
And taste the perfume of her glowing flowers,
　Dim as forget-me-nots in summer rain.''

Edna Jaques

Summer Wishes

Summer suns, shine gently here;
Summer breeze, blow soft and clear:
Keep my garden fresh and fair
So the hours run smoothly there.

Summer stars, shine softly down;
Evening, trail your perfumed gown.
Fairy fingers, gently stray;
Elfin pipers, softly play.

Misty haze of summer dawn,
Gently touch this velvet lawn.
May this spot a haven be
For bird and butterfly and bee.

Elizabeth Oliver Leichliter

Wide Front Porch

People who live in cities never know
The creak of hickory rockers and the hum
Of talk about what happened years ago.
Those who planned farmsteads hereabouts took time
Enough to square a beam and see it placed;
A man of sixty wasn't past his prime,
And nothing worth a penny went to waste.
We can remember many things with pride,
Who built front porches neighborly and wide.

Leslie N. Jennings

The Old Porch Swing

I remember summer evenings
In the old porch swing,
With all the warm nostalgia
Which childhood memories bring.
The street lamps gently flickered,
Casting shadows on the grass,
As the family sat and chatted
And watched the people pass.
The fireflies in the cannas
Made spangles in the dark,
While just around the corner
We could hear a hound dog bark.
There were happy calls from children
As they wandered home from play,
And the crickets chirped softly
In a summer roundelay.
That's why an evening's twilight
Sets me to remembering
Those sweet and tender moments
I spent in that old porch swing.

Mary Ellen Stelling

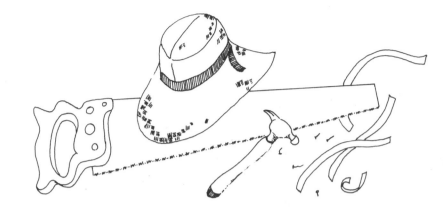

Refinisher
of Furniture

"Refinisher of Furniture"—
This sign upon his wall
Cannot describe the talent rare
That makes him known to all.

He has an eye for loveliness
And lines of charm and grace
In furniture long cast aside
As new styles found their place.

The love seats and the oak buffets
So treasured years ago,
He renders useful once again
With all their former glow.

He does his work most thoroughly
With hours of toil and care
For every curved-glass China hutch
Or stately rocking chair.

And when his patient diligence
At last has found a form,
He'll have restored both furniture
And memories warm.

Craig E. Sathoff

Photo opposite
BROOM-MAKER
Ina Mackey

Playing Checkers at the General Store

In a dim nook partly sheltered by the
Barrels therein stored,
With rapt, intent expressions, sit two
Players at the board;
And the country merchant lingers,
Loath to serve the public more,
For his thoughts are with the worthies
Playing checkers at the store.

Pondering the situation on the mimic
Battlefield,
Guarding carefully the "king row"
Lest the small battalion yield,
"Jumping" with a gleeful chuckle,
Crowning his opponent's "king,"
Each man slowly and with caution plots
His maneuvering.

Even the supper hour approaching
With its promise of good cheer
Has no magic in its summons to entice
The players here.
Yet the contest at its finish through some
Fine unwritten law
May with all its complications be
Decided by a "draw."

Some may boast of golf and tennis and
The tournaments of chess,
Heralded by great announcements
And plaudits of the press,
But such champions of pleasure with
Their fund of players' lore
Well might envy these old worthies
Playing checkers at the store.

Lois Mae Cuhel

Overleaf
GARDEN DELIGHTS
Gay Bumgarner

Timeless Mackinac Island

Time slows to a crawl as the ferryboat chugs its way gradually through the churning waters of Lake Michigan toward the tiny, isolated tract of land known as Mackinac Island. Rising like an aged, green turtle from the chilly waters of the lake, Mackinac offers its many visitors a slower, simpler lifestyle—a welcome relief from the hectic pace of modern mainland life.

Gulls screech and whirl over the piers where ferries dock several times each day to unload passengers from the mainland. There is no bridge or highway to Mackinac, nor is there need for one. Shortly after the invention of the automobile in 1876, the town fathers banned the noisy contraptions from the island—and the ban still stands today. Visitors must walk, ride bicycles, or enjoy horse-drawn carts and carriages as they explore the treasures hidden on Mackinac's shores and hillsides.

As lake breezes freshen the summer air, a walk down the main thoroughfare has its effect on even the most seasoned traveler. Bunches of bright-eyed daisies nod and smile from the arms of a corner vendor. Little shops standing side by side offer unique gifts from Mackinac's past and present: wood and crystal wrought in intricate shapes and scenes—an Indian canoe, a French trapper with his catch, an eighteenth century schooner. Perhaps one of the island's greatest temptations, however, is its famous fudge. The rich aroma of chocolate and caramel entices even determined dieters; the summer folk who frequent the confectioneries are nicknamed "fudgies" by the local residents.

Above the busy shops, rising on a grassy knoll a few blocks from the waterfront, is the restored Mackinac fort. It hosted French, British, and American troops in its colorful past and became part of Mackinac National Park in 1875. Since then, the buildings and parade grounds have undergone extensive renovation, and today a history buff will find many fascinating nooks and crannies to explore.

The fur trade that brought John Jacob Astor's American Fur Company to Mackinac in the mid-1800s drew others there as well, and it wasn't long before the beautiful island had cast its spell and determined its destiny as a tranquil escape from the hectic pace of city life. American poet William Cullen Bryant eloquently noted, "The world has not many islands so beautiful as Mackinac."

Despite this richness of natural beauty, no trip to Mackinac would be complete without a visit to the Grand Hotel. Built over a century ago, it crowns the limestone hillside above the tiny town. The velvety emerald lawns and beautifully manicured gardens provide an exquisite setting for the luxurious white clapboard "palace." Overlooking the terrace and pool is the geranium-bedecked verandah of the world's longest porch. Its famous 880-foot length is the scene of one of Mackinac's few sporting events—one eminently suited to the island's pace—the World's Sauntering Championships! Each August contestants traverse the length of the verandah, and the last to finish is declared the winner!

But the Grand offers more sublime pleasures as well. In the richness of the softly lit lobby one may take afternoon tea served in fragile china cups and accompanied by the soothing strains of Bach and Chopin. Here the mind and heart may escape today and wander, unencumbered, to a calm and quieter past.

It seems as though the passage of time slows and even reverses as one experiences the varied textures of this tiny island. Mackinac weaves a tapestry of history and romance, drawing tones from sky and water, earth and star. She beckons us with her grace and charm and promises to give us something as elusive as a summer breeze—a taste of yesterday.

Pamela Kennedy

Old-Fashioned Confections

BUTTER NUT CRUNCH

1 cup sugar
½ teaspoon salt
¼ cup water
½ cup butter

½ teaspoon lecithin, optional
½ cup nuts
3 cups chocolate chips, melted

Combine sugar, salt, water, butter, and lecithin in a heavy skillet or saucepan. Cook mixture until candy thermometer registers 285°. Add nuts. Remove from heat. Pour onto well-greased cookie sheet; cool. Spread half of melted chocolate on the cooled candy. Sprinkle with half of nuts. When the chocolate is firm, turn the candy over on waxed paper and spread with remaining melted chocolate. Sprinkle with remaining nuts. Break into pieces when firm. Makes about 20 pieces.

CREAMY BUTTER FUDGE

3 cups granulated sugar
½ cup cocoa
⅛ teaspoon salt
1 tablespoon unflavored gelatin
1 cup whipping cream
½ cup milk

¼ cup light corn syrup
½ cup butter
½ cup margarine
1½ teaspoons vanilla
1½ cups chopped walnuts or pecans

Combine all ingredients, except vanilla and nuts, in heavy 4-quart saucepan; blend well. Bring to rolling boil, stirring constantly. Continue cooking until candy thermometer registers 238°; gradually lower heat and stir gently. Remove from heat; pour into bowl. Cool 20 minutes; add vanilla and beat with mixer on low speed until creamy. Stir in nuts. Spread in 9-inch square pan. Cool and cut into squares. Makes about 50 pieces.

PEANUT BUTTER CARAMELS

½ cup chopped peanuts or pecans
½ cup smooth peanut butter
2½ cups granulated sugar
¾ cup light corn syrup

6 tablespoons butter
⅛ teaspoon salt
½ teaspoon lecithin, optional
2 cups whipping cream

Butter a 9-inch square pan. Sprinkle nuts over bottom of pan. Combine peanut butter, granulated sugar, corn syrup, butter, salt, lecithin, and 1 cup whipping cream in heavy 3-quart saucepan. Bring to boil over medium heat, stirring constantly. Gradually add remaining 1 cup cream when mixture is at a full rolling boil. Continue to stir, lowering heat as mixture thickens, until candy thermometer registers 245°. Remove from heat. Pour mixture over nuts. Cool. When firm cut into squares. Makes about 60 pieces.

Photo opposite
OLD-FASHIONED CONFECTIONS
Gerald Koser

The CHARLIE McCARTHY Show

During the heyday of live radio in the 1930s and '40s, families gathered together in the living room to listen to exciting and timely broadcasts, including FDR's famous "fireside chats," the suspense of "The Saint," and numerous comedy hours. Will Rogers, political satirist of the time, the ever-modest Jack Benny, the comic duo of George Burns and Gracie Allen, and the unforgettable "Amos 'n' Andy" characters all offered hours of listening pleasure to their spellbound audiences.

Sunday nights at eight o'clock held the most appeal for many Americans. With the evening meal's dishes neatly stacked and toys in their places, Father settled into his comfy chair and gathered the family around the radio in anticipation of another hilarious episode in the lives of "Edgar Bergen and Charlie McCarthy."

This duo was not actually two people, as the name implies, but a ventriloquist and his dummy. Bergen played the role of the calm and patient adult defending the values of his society. Charlie, his wooden sidekick, portrayed the saucy, pleasure-seeking teenager we all hate, but secretly love. Each dressed his part, too. Bergen donned a relatively conservative tweed suit and tie, and sported carefully slicked hair. Charlie, on the other hand, flaunted a dapper tuxedo complete with shiny top hat, white bow tie, and a starched white shirt. He even paraded a monocle on his puffed right cheek, framing his youthful, perky eye.

Their routine usually consisted of Bergen attempting to teach Charlie the ways of the world, as well as proper etiquette — with disastrous results. His soft, paternal words of sense and experience fell on deaf wooden ears as Charlie sassily rebuked such worthless, boring advice. This banter was primarily carried on through plays on words with Charlie tossing out stinging asides every now and then about Bergen's mindlessness, thinning hair, and moving mouth.

Charlie was modeled after a young Irish newsboy of Bergen's high school days. Theodore Mack, a carpenter, carved the dummy who was destined to become America's ill-mannered but beloved child, Charlie. In tribute to the carpenter and the newsboy, Bergen shortened the carpenter's surname to "Mc" and added a Celtic ending, "Carthy," to come up with Charlie's last name.

Through his amateur shows with Charlie, Bergen made his way through college where he was aspiring to enter the field of medicine. But instead of pursuing this goal, Bergen decided to try the vaudeville circuit. After a decade of meager success with journeys to Europe, Russia, and South America under his belt, Charlie returned to America's stage as we now know him — a bit more refined in a freshly-pressed tux and smooth British accent. The duo's appearance on Rudy Vallee's "Royal Gelatin Hour" in 1936 catapulted their career. In 1937, NBC offered Bergen and McCarthy their own show, "The Chase and Sanborn Hour," changed later to "The Charlie McCarthy Show," as the talkative dummy scooted aside his human partner and became a star. Such was the popularity of this little smart-aleck that first-rate personalities in the entertainment business like Mae West, Marilyn Monroe, and W. C. Fields often dropped by the studio to trade insults with him.

In time, Bergen also added two more dummies to his act. The first, Mortimer Snerd, depicted a simpleton from the country in desperate need of orthodontal attention. Whereas Bergen assumed the role of father to his dummies, Mortimer stirred a protective maternal instinct in his listeners. Effie, forming the last character in the quartet, was the lonely busybody of the radio station, always on the lookout for a possible mate.

In just this way, a man with his trio of characters entertained America throughout the '40s and mid '50s, bringing delight to a nation that struggled through economic hardship and war and still could laugh at itself.

Kathy Halgren

A PLEASANT MEMORY

Oh, what a thrill it was to meet
An organ grinder on the street,
And as he passed along the way,
He always brightened up my day.

I loved to hear his happy song
And watch his monkey dance along,
And, oh, I'd clap my hands in glee
When he would play a tune for me!

The little monkey held a cup
And waited while folks filled it up
With nickels, dimes and pennies, too —
Then tipped his hat when they were through.

Although today I'd like to meet
An organ grinder on the street,
The organ grinder is to me
Now just a pleasant memory!

Patricia Mongeau

Photo opposite
HURDY GURDY MAN
Arnold Kaplan
Berg & Associates

Readers' Reflections

Bouquet on the Bookshelf

Deep in a darkened corner
On the shelf among my books,
Waiting to be discovered
By anyone who looks,

Is a little bunch of daisies
In a shiny copper bowl
Where they brighten up the shadows
On the shelf and in my soul.

Yes, they're artificial,
But they're fashioned with such care
That they seem as fresh and pretty
As real flowers sitting there.

Daisies blooming by the roadside
In the summer are so dear,
But the bouquet on the bookshelf
Lifts my spirits all the year.

Donna R. Skeid
Rayland, Ohio

Lamplight

Before the age of energy —
With light in every room —
Folks used the light of kerosene
To dispel the dark and gloom.

When an evening rain descended
And the air was cool and damp,
We gathered inside Grandma's house,
And she lit the old oil lamp.

We sat around the table;
Grandma made a pot of tea.
In the cheerful glow of lamplight,
It was cozy as could be!

The rain beat hard upon the roof
In the world outside so drear —
Love and warmth wrapped folks inside
With peace and an inner cheer.

Carol E. Williams
Beloit, Ohio

Editor's Note: Readers are invited to submit poetry, short anecdotes, and humorous reflections on life for possible publication in future *Ideals* issues. Please send xeroxed copies only; manuscripts will not be returned. Writers will receive $10 for each published submission. Send material to "Readers' Reflections," P.O. Box 1101, Milwaukee, Wisconsin 53201.

Old-Fashioned Things

I love old-fashioned things: peonies pink and
Roses white, long hair catching candlelight,
Crystal beads and old gold rings —
How I love old-fashioned things!

Oh, give me the old-fashioned things:
A homey room with winding stairs, old stained
Glass, a rocking chair, soft rag rugs in colors
Bright, the ticking clock, an oil lamp's light,
Rain on the rooftop pattering away, sweetest
Smell of new-mown hay, old barns where small
Kittens stay, the way the whirling windmill
Sings — I never tire of old-fashioned things.

Just let me hear a waltz of old, share the sunsets
Orange and gold, take delight when friends drop by,
Bake them bread and apple pie, dine to the song my
Teapot sings — I love old-fashioned things.

Rose Emily Houston
Hendersonville, North Carolina

A Mixture of Things

Life can be
    a mixture of things —
A garden of tulips,
    freshwater springs,
Fluffy white clouds,
    stars in blue sky,
A sunrise at dawn,
    a mountain so high,
A rugged rail fence,
    a soft, gentle breeze,
A trellis of roses,
    a child on his knees,
A cat with her kittens,
    a butterfly's wings —
Life can be
    a mixture of things.

Mabel Ielene Rathmann
Sugar Creek, Missouri

Overleaf
BARNUM & BAILEY CIRCUS
Three Lions

THE CIRCUS DRUMS

I saw the circus parade today;
I heard the great big bass drums play,
And I understand what they tried to say.

"Come — come to the circus," they said,
"And watch the elephant stand on his head,
And the little white poodle pretend he's dead.

"See the bareback riders that jump through a hoop,
And the man in the auto that loops the loop,
And the monkey that eats a bowl of soup.

"There will be ladies in sparkly gowns,
And men on trapezes, and tumbling clowns,
And a lion tamer that scolds and frowns."

That's what the big drums said, although
It only sounded like "boom," I know,
But I understood and I'm going to go!

Adelaide Love

From *Child Life Magazine*, copyright 1938, 1966 by Rand McNally & Company.
Reprinted with permission of the publisher.

CIRCUS PARADE

It comes! It comes!
Down the street at last
to calliope melody
and the clowns' shenanigans
with the ponderous heavy
plodding of elephants
and the keepers shouting
and the creaking of
heavy wheels under the
cages of lion and tiger
and circus ladies
riding the silken horses
and the smell of animals
in the heat, and popcorn,
and balloons popping.
And the parade is more fun
than anything later on
under the big top!

Elizabeth Searle Lamb

Carousel

Of all the circus rides that cast a spell,
I still prefer the wondrous carousel.
With brightly painted steeds all set to run,
The gay calliope begins the fun.

The ponies gallop gracefully around,
With flashing hooves that never touch the ground,
And soar with ease toward a spangled night,
In prancing manner and ecstatic flight.

The music stops. The ponies stand quite still,
With flaring nostrils, flashing eyes, until
It starts again, and then, away they go!
Up, down; up, down — too many times to know!

Roy Kemp

Elsie Natalie Brady

Elsie Natalie Brady, a native of New Jersey, has written over 300 poems, many reflecting her love of nature. Her work has appeared in a variety of publications and church bulletins across the country.

She has received recognition for her prose, as well. In 1963 she won a set of *The Great Books of the Western World* for writing a letter of general interest in a contest sponsored by Dr. Mortimer J. Adler. Her topic was "Happiness." This, too, is reflected in her poems, especially those with an old-fashioned flavor.

Our Parlor

The parlor was a special room
That we would seldom see,
Except when visitors would come
And stay for cakes and tea.

The sliding doors were opened wide
For each festive holiday;
With wonderment we'd go inside
To pass the time away.

The ornate sofa and tall chairs
Were trimmed with bits of lace
That Mom crocheted with loving care
For old-world charm and grace.

And our old piano, polished bright,
Helped make the rafters ring
When we joined in with much delight
The happy songs to sing.

The Old Front Porch

Our old front porch . . . I can see it still,
Just as it used to be,
Embracing the house at the foot of the hill,
Waiting for company.

It is older now, but yet as strong
As it was when we were young,
But the honeysuckle vines are gone
And the wind-chimes' tinkling song.

The porch was always a cheerful place,
With flowers and rocking chairs.
It had old-world charm, with handmade lace
Under vases and souvenirs.

Sometimes, we stop to visit awhile
With the folks now living there,
And the porch seems to greet us with a smile,
As happy memories we share.

The Wooden Tub

Our wooden tub was big and round,
With metal bands securely bound.
On Mondays, it was full of suds
For washing sheets and family duds.

We also bathed in it each week
Behind a drape, so none might peek;
And, once, into the tub were thrown
Some large blue crabs that Dad brought home.

To us it was a needed friend
Of many uses without end,
But that was many years ago,
When life was leisurely and slow.

The Umbrella Man

The umbrella man was a usual sight
In the not-so-long-ago.
Children would follow him with delight
As he wandered to and fro.

He carried a grindstone upon his back —
Knives and scissors he'd sharpen, too —
Of customers there was seldom a lack,
He always had something to do.

"Umbrellas to mend, umbrellas to mend,"
He would sing as he trudged along.
Through many a sleepy town he'd wend
His way with a happy song.

The Beloved Doctor

I remember our doctor's house calls
Which he made by day and by night,
The bruises he tended from bumps and falls
With ointments and bandages white.

He would know what to do for a fever
To ease the discomfort and pain,
And he was a most ardent believer
In potions that brought health again.

So often a small gift he'd carry
To a child who was long ill in bed,
And with him awhile he would tarry.
For payment, he'd accept homemade bread,

And seemed to forget what was owed him
When some folks could not pay their bills;
Instead, with gratis bestowed them
The tonics and unguents and pills.

His coming made us feel better;
His smile banished worry and gloom;
He always brought sunshiny weather
Into every patient's sickroom.

The Old Wooden Trolley

In the good old horse and buggy days,
Folks travelled near and far
In horse-drawn carriages and shays
And in wooden trolley car.

A motorman, with waxed moustache,
Would steer the car along,
And make the change, and take the cash,
And pull the iron gong.

An electric wire overhead
Fed a temperamental rod
Atop the trolley as it sped
On tracks in stone and sod.

On holidays, suave gentlemen
Would take their ladies fair
Aboard the trolley for a spin
And a breath of country air.

The trolley now is seldom seen,
And with its passing went
An era that was more serene
And also more content.

Midsummer Day

The fairy folk were out last night,
　　All through the air a-dancing,
'Neath shifting rays of soft starlight,
　　O'er dewy meadows prancing.

They emptied out the lily's cup,
　　Its choicest nectar keeping,
The bees and birds were wakened up,
　　And so, today, they're sleeping.

The leaves are still, the winds are hushed,
　　Only the sun is shining —
For every cloud away has rushed
　　To polish up its lining.

All Mother Nature is asleep today,
　　In spite of old Sol's beaming;
The hotter he sends down his rays,
　　The deeper is her dreaming.

Oh, flowers and singing birds and bees,
　　What very lazy creatures,
To seek the shelter of the trees
　　And hide your sleepy features.

The Year is at its very crest,
　　And Earth and Air together
Are pausing for a little rest,
　　This sweet midsummer weather.

　　　　　　　Martha L. Hood

Photo opposite
MIDSUMMER MAGIC
Bob Coyle

Country Chronicle

Lansing Christman

Memories of the old-fashioned ways of country life are rekindled in these long rich hours of summertime. Those iron kettles one sees on rural lawns bring back nostalgic recollections of an era of an earlier time on the farms of the nation. Many implements and household items used as recently as fifty years ago have become antiques, relics of the past, symbols of our heritage and ingenuity.

Those iron kettles, for instance, were used in boiling down the sap of maple trees into syrup and sugar. They were used for boiling water at butchering time, and for heating water for the routine washing of clothing. Some of them now serve as yard ornaments, or as rustic containers for beds of flowers.

In this benevolent season of sun and warmth, a man remembers the weeks spent in the harvesting of hay from the meadows, with the unforgettable aroma of timothy curing and drying in the swathes where it fell before the rhythmic clicking knives of the mower's cutting bar. He remembers the horse-drawn mowing machine and the vital role it played on his steep acres. Nor will he forget the big team of grays with swishing tails pulling the clattering, cumbersome machine as he made trip after trip around fields bathed in sunlight. The mower had its companion, the hay rake, with its long, curved teeth which would rattle and clang as it moved over the new-mown hay, raking the timothy into windrows, reaching like outstretched arms across the meadow.

Inside the man's barn there are other relics of the past. Burnished by a century of summer and winter weather, a cradle used long ago in the harvest of grain hangs near the empty granary. Its bent wooden shaft and handles glisten like gold when the light of day streams in through an opened door. Nearby, a neck yoke and horse collars hang on nails driven into the rough-hewn wall.

The wagon house, built as a residence in the 1700s, is now a haven for the chattering barn swallows which dive and swoop in and around the slanting rafters where they have plastered their mud-like nests. The building still bears strips of wallpaper that decorated the rooms from that earlier era when people inhabited it.

The man's grandfather, in the mid 1860s, initiated the construction of a new house, which also holds treasures of bygone days. The parlor carpet has covered the floor through the greater part of three generations in a family line. There are horsehair chairs, a sofa, and a corner whatnot with its trinkets dating back to other times. A grandfather's clock still chimes the hours away.

A man was intimately associated with old-fashioned machinery and tools and implements in the earlier years of this century as he worked the rugged land. Today's modern equipment and conveniences ease the work of both the tiller of the soil and the rural housewife. What once were tools of the trade have now been relegated to museums and antique shops, to cellars and attics and parlors, to weathered barns and sheds — reminders of a past way of American life that a man still cherishes in his memories.

To Be
a Child Again

Oh, the joys to be found in an old rail fence
And the treasures hidden there
Bring fond recollections of childhood days
And a life both rich and rare.

We would sit on the fence and, by stretching high,
Reach up in the apple tree
Where the snowy white blossoms so fragrantly sweet
Would brush o'er our cheeks fleetingly.

In a snug little corner so safe and warm
Where soft, gentle breezes pass,
We would find the spot where a sly mother bird
Had built her nest in the grass.

A little brown toad, looking just like the earth,
Underneath a white toadstool
Sat, blinking his eyes and looking content,
Where the ground was moist and cool.

A jack-in-the-pulpit, so straight and tall,
Stood as if ready to preach.
Adder's-tongues, violets, mayflowers, too,
Were all there within our reach.

Oh, the treasures we found 'neath the old rail fence
Are ever as bright and new,
And the golden days of a childhood fair
Are still waiting there for you!

Evelyn G. Gahlau

Photo opposite
SUNFLOWERS
H. Armstrong Roberts

He Didn't Want Him Any Smaller

Beside the open door he stood,
Shyly, and somewhat aloof,
While the burly blacksmith pared
The sturdy pony's hoof.

His misgivings at last found voice,
And his form grew two inches taller.
"Please stop that, Mr. Smith," he cried,
"I don't want him any smaller."

Frank H. Stauffer

Old Barns

I like the smell of an old barn:
The milk-sweet breath of cows,
The pungency of hay, the scent of horses.
In corners, sunbeams spin the hay to yarn
Of fabled gold; new kittens drowse;
The ever-present Plymouth Rock discourses
On subjects interesting to a hen —
Her lazy chatter rousing in the mind
Childhood's enchantment with the new-filled mow —
That in a flash changed from a robbers' den
To haunted house, to patriots' fort, behind
Whose bristling walls we shouted threat and vow;
Or, as we climbed the ladder, it became
A pirate ship that sailed imperiled seas
Through mountainous waves around the Southern Horn,
Ringing with salty echoes of our game.

Fast disappearing, time's discourtesies
Have left the few remaining lean and worn
On isolated hillsides; sway-backed, gray,
They speak in mournful accents to the wind,
And these are the words they seem to say —
Their ancient voices high and thinned —
Long, long ago and far away . . . .

Marion Doyle

Hay Wagon

Here, where the road goes winding on its way
And the gold haze of afternoon hangs warm,
A creaking wagon loaded high with hay
Makes the old pilgrimage from field to farm.

The agile vehicles, more swiftly paced,
Come up behind and angered passers-by,
With churning engines, blow their horns of haste,
Filling the country road with hue and cry.

Lazing, the driver scarcely seems to heed
As from his seat he pulls a languid rein
And lets them pass — like one averse to speed
Who lives within a steadier domain.

For here the scented air is drowsy-sweet.
The feathered wisps brush gently on the ground
Or cling to branches. Let us pause to meet
The year's abundant harvest, homeward bound.

Helen Frith Stickney

Pigeons in an Old Mill

Silent now, the windmill is at rest;
The sun makes patterns on the dusty floor;
A rustling, cooing sound comes from a nest;
A wanton wind sighs through an oaken door.
In and out through open windows fly
The pigeons, their blue-green throats a-quiver;
Home they come through crimson, sunset sky
To the old windmill beside the river.

Life is kind to restless things that soar,
Happy in their world of living free.
Wings unbound, they know no alien shore —
They spurn fetters and captivity.
Swiftly winging homeward, they display
Shadows of some far-off yesterday.

Irene Archer

Loyalty, Peace, Integrity

I like rooms furnished in old-time things:
Brass and pewter and prim-flowered chintz,
A seasoned fire that whispers and sings,
Ruffled curtains and Godey prints,
Soft rag rugs that with loving care
Grandmother worked on all year round,
A gate-legged table, a high-backed chair,
A grandfather clock with deep, rich sound,
A sofa with pillows plumped with care,
Special to us for its years of wear.

I like souls furnished in time-tried things:
Honor and faith and a sense of sin,
Courage and truth and a hope that brings
Good cheer without and strength within,
Loyalty, peace, and integrity,
A decent regard for the Sabbath day.
Virtues ennobling you and me,
Those we can all live with, come what may,
Virtues that steady and satisfy —
Our fathers trusted them. So do I.

Nonee Nolan

Old Things

I love old things, old books, old friends,
　　The lovely way an old tree bends
Above a little clapboard house,
　　A tiny yard still as a mouse,

A zig-zag fence of cedar rails,
　　A stout old ship with mended sails,
Tall trees around a village square,
　　A chest of thin old silverware,

I love the sheen of oaken floors,
　　Wrought iron hinges on old doors,
The sound that flowing water makes,
　　The weathered brown of cedar shakes.

I love old things, timeworn and frayed,
　　Upon whose heart the years have laid
A kindly touch as if to show
　　The beauty of their inner glow.

Edna Jaques

Ideals Takes to the Roads

Join us for an autumn stroll in ou[r] next issue, Country Roads.

Let our beautiful color photograph[s] and inspiring poetry and prose sti[r] the gypsy in your soul. Or just sit atop the old rail fence warming your heart with fall's flames of gol[d] and crimson. Either way, you'll travel the byways from country to town and back again — just in tim[e] to sample one of our delicious apple desserts.

For a little excitement along the way, ride with us through legendary Sleepy Hollow on Halloween night.

But, don't come alone! Bring your family and friends. There's no bett[er] way to share the colors of autumn[,] or the tranquility of Country Road[s] than with a gift subscription to Ideals.

ACKNOWLEDGMENTS

OLD BARNS by Marion Doyle from TED MALONE'S ADVENTURES IN POETRY, [copy]right 1946 by William Morrow and Company, Inc.; MIDSUMMER DAY by Martha L. [...] from FROM MY WINDOW; TO AN OLD FARMHOUSE from BESIDE STILL WATER[S] [by] Edna Jaques, copyright 1939 by Thomas Allen, Limited; OLD THINGS from THE GO[LDEN] ROAD by Edna Jaques, copyright 1953 by Thomas Allen, Limited; CIRCUS PARAD[E by] Elizabeth Searle Lamb originally published in *Capper's Weekly*; THE DAYS GON[E] from RHYMES OF CHILDHOOD, copyright 1890, 1898, 1900 by James Whitcomb [Riley,] Bobbs-Merrill Company, Publishers; HE DIDN'T WANT HIM ANY SMALLER by Fra[nk H.] Stauffer from HARPER'S YOUNG PEOPLE, copyright 1889 by Harper & Row, Publis[hers;] WHEN SHE MUST GO by Margaret Widdemer from 1,000 INSPIRATIONAL THINGS, [copy]right 1948 by The Spencer Press, Inc.; AN AWFUL LOT TO FISHIN' by R. C. Calle[n,] WIDE FRONT PORCH by Leslie N. Jennings, A MORTIFYING MISTAKE by Anna [M.] Pratt, and HAY WAGON by Helen Frith Stickney all from THE DESK DRAWER ANT[HOL]OGY, copyright 1927 by Doubleday, Doran, & Company, Inc.; recipe for BUTTER [...] CRUNCH from CANDY COOKBOOK, copyright © 1979 by Mildred Brand, publish[ed by] Ideals Publishing Corporation; recipes for CREAMY BUTTER FUDGE and PEANUT [BUT]TER CARAMELS from CANDY AND CANDY MOLDING COOKBOOK, copyright © 19[79 by] Mildred Brand, published by Ideals Publishing Corporation. Our sincere thanks [to the] following authors whose addresses we were unable to locate: Irene Archer for PIGE[ONS] IN AN OLD MILL, Lois Mae Cuhel for PLAYING CHECKERS AT THE GENERAL ST[ORE,] Elizabeth Oliver Leichliter for SUMMER WISHES, Margaret Neel for THE FLOU[R...] Nonee Nolan for LOYALTY, PEACE, INTEGRITY, and Ruth Linnea Erickson for GR[AND]GRANDMOTHER'S KITCHEN from HOMESPUN VERSE. copyright 1956 by Ruth L[innea] Erickson, published by Rollinson & Hey.